GREEN CITIES

How Green Infrastructure Helps Urban Centers Thrive

Written by
SHEILA BOUDREAU

Illustrated by
KATY DOCKRILL

Owlkids Books

This book is dedicated to my three children, Gareth, Evan, and Cate, with the hope that their love of Mother Earth will continue to bring them joy throughout their lives —**S.B.**

To all who plant—bringing shade, fresh air, and beauty, even in the smallest spaces —**K.D.**

Owlkids Books acknowledges the financial support of the Canada Council for the Arts, the Ontario Arts Council, the Government of Canada through the Canada Book Fund (CBF) and the Government of Ontario through the Ontario Creates Book Initiative for our publishing activities.

Owlkids Books gratefully acknowledges that our office in Toronto is located on the traditional territory of many nations, including the Mississaugas of the Credit, the Chippewa, the Wendat, the Anishinaabeg, and the Haudenosaunee Peoples.

Published in Canada by Owlkids Books Inc., 1 Eglinton Avenue East, Toronto, ON M4P 3A1
Published in the US by Owlkids Books Inc., 819 Bancroft Way, Berkeley, CA 94710

Library of Congress Control Number: 2025939356

Library and Archives Canada Cataloguing in Publication
Title: Green cities : how green infrastructure helps urban centers thrive / written by Sheila Boudreau ; illustrated by Katy Dockrill.
Names: Boudreau, Sheila, author. | Dockrill, Katy, illustrator
Description: Includes bibliographical references and index.
Identifiers: Canadiana (print) 20250215500 | Canadiana (ebook) 20250215519 | ISBN 9781771476072 (hardcover) | ISBN 9781771477710 (EPUB)
Subjects: LCSH: City planning—Environmental aspects—Juvenile literature. | LCSH: Sustainable urban development—Juvenile literature. | LCSH: Sustainable living—Juvenile literature. | LCSH: City and town life—Juvenile literature.
Classification: LCC HT166 .B68 2026 | DDC j307.1/216—dc23

Edited by Stacey Roderick | Designed by Alisa Baldwin

Manufactured in Shenzhen, Guangdong, China, in August 2025, by C & C Offset
Job #HZ2091

hc A B C D E F

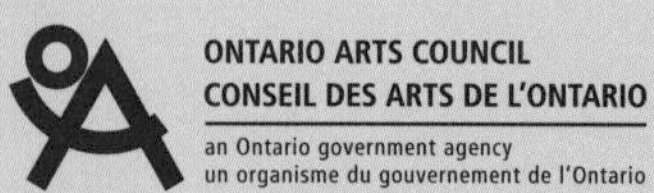

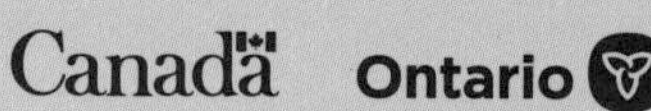

CONTENTS

INTRODUCTION

A Green Way

When you think of a city, you probably picture a busy, noisy place filled with paved streets, concrete sidewalks, and buildings of all kinds. It's easy to forget that before there was a city, there was nature. In fact, nature is *still* there. And although you might not realize it, it is a very important part of our cities.

For instance, have you ever walked from a busy city street into a park filled with trees on a hot day? The cool, fresh air is such a relief from the steamy sidewalks and shadeless roads! Whether that park was specially created or was once a forest that the city grew around, it's an example of nature's power to transform an urban environment.

And guess what! We can make use of nature's incredible powers by designing our cities to include something called green infrastructure.

Infrastructure is what we call the system of human-engineered parts that keep a city running smoothly and safely. Traditional gray infrastructure, like paved roads, bridges, and underground sewers, is made of concrete, metal, and even plastic. Green infrastructure, on the other hand, makes use of the living things that grow and thrive in an urban environment, such as trees and plants. It also includes human-made systems that are inspired by or designed to work with nature, such as green roofs (specially designed roof ecosystems) and permeable paving (pavement that lets water run through into the earth below).

The great news is that many city-builders are now including green infrastructure in their plans. Why? Because a green city is more livable and plays an important role in addressing climate change. As you will see in this book, lots of exciting projects around the world are harnessing nature's power to make cities that are great to live in and can help protect Earth's future. And you will discover ways that you, your family, your friends and classmates can get involved in making *your* city greener too!

"As a human family we need to work deliberately at harmony. That is what the Earth requires. Harmony is the energy that heals."

—RICHARD WAGAMESE,
Ojibwe author and poet,
Wabaseemoong First Nation

CHAPTER 1

Cities:
A Great Invention that Could Be Even Better

Around the world, people like to live close to one another in permanent settlements, from smaller towns to sprawling cities. It might seem like a modern idea, but humans have lived together in this way for over fourteen thousand years!

The earliest cities started out as small villages that grew as more people moved from the countryside. Some of the first cities had tall walls and earthen barriers to protect those who lived there from wild animals and invaders, especially during times of war.

As urban populations grew, problems such as crowded living conditions needed to be addressed. For example, to make sure that people had drinking water, some cities built aboveground channels (called aqueducts) to take clean water from higher areas down to those living in lower areas. Drainage systems were needed to direct stormwater and stinky sewage to underground trenches that led away from areas where people lived. Bridges were sometimes built across rivers, and road systems were added to allow people to travel more quickly by foot, on horse, or in vehicles. All these things are part of the structures and services we call infrastructure.

These growing cities also needed to provide large areas that people could use as gathering places and as outdoor markets to sell food and other goods. And with so many people moving in, cities became places for sharing new ideas and for learning too. Soon there was a need for schools, colleges, and universities. In fact, some of the world's oldest cities are considered birthplaces of the arts and sciences. Hospitals were also built to help meet the health needs of these bigger populations.

The early cities had to expand beyond their original boundaries as more and more people moved in. And this is still happening today, with modern cities taking over more land to fit growing numbers of people and businesses. More than half of the people in the world live in urban environments, and this number is rising fast!

With cities taking up increasing amounts of space around the world, it's important that we design and build them in a way that protects the health of those who live there—and the health of the planet we call home.

Some **ANCIENT ROMAN BRIDGES** were designed as both aqueducts to carry clean water to cities and pedestrian crossings. A few were built so well, they are still being used today.
The oldest known permanent city is thought to be **SHEDET**, on the Nile River in Egypt. It was established around 4000 BCE. People still live there today, in a *much* more modern city called Faiyum.

What Does City Planning Have to Do with Infrastructure?

Imagine trying to build something as big and complicated as a city without having a plan. Not a good idea, right?

No two modern cities are exactly alike, but in all cities, land is used for a variety of purposes, including residential (houses and apartment buildings), institutional (schools, hospitals, and buildings for worship), industrial (factories), and commercial (stores and restaurants). Cities also need land for roads, public transportation systems, and airports, and for open spaces like parks and other natural areas. And they need

CITY PLANNING is the process of creating an overall long-term design—including the infrastructure. It considers who owns and is responsible for the land, who will care for the natural areas, and what the needs and wishes of those who live there are.

land for the systems that help keep the city livable and safe—in other words, the infrastructure. These include water systems (for drinking water, sewage, and stormwater) and utilities (like electricity, natural gas, and communications systems). A city's plan makes sure all these parts work well together.

Urban planners also keep track of a city's population density, which is the number of people living in a given area of land. Planners make sure that there is enough space for a particular land use, such as housing or factories, and that people have access to the services they need.

There are many parts of a city and many different needs to be met, so careful planning is critical. Green infrastructure is a key part of that planning because we know that cities both contribute to and experience the effects of climate change in significant ways.

THE 15-MINUTE CITY

One green city-planning concept is the 15-minute city (also called the walkable city). The idea is that people should be able to walk to key services such as grocery stores, doctors, and schools in no more than fifteen minutes. When cities add nature along the way, the experience becomes more enjoyable and encourages people to walk instead of drive. This is good not only for people's physical and mental health but also for the planet.

Cities and Climate Change

Our planet is getting hotter. And as it heats up, the world is experiencing more extreme and unusual weather events, such as stronger hurricanes and severe heat waves. We call this process climate change.

Climate change is happening because some human activities—especially ones that burn fossil fuels such as coal and oil—are increasing the amount of carbon dioxide (CO_2) and other gases within Earth's atmosphere. These gases (sometimes called greenhouse gases) then form a kind of barrier that traps more heat. This is known as the greenhouse effect.

You might be surprised to learn that cities produce *over 70 percent* of the world's greenhouse gases! This isn't just because there are so many people living and working in them. It's mainly because of *how* we build and run them. In fact, just the way concrete is made and used contributes to the problem, from the energy required to the greenhouse gases that are produced. Or imagine all

GREEN INFRASTRUCTURE is a nature-based solution, which means it works with natural systems and processes to prevent and lessen the effects of climate change, while also supporting biodiversity. This term was coined by the International Union for Conservation of Nature, a group made up of Indigenous Peoples, governments, and other organizations.

the large machines and trucks needed to clear space for and construct a city's gray infrastructure and buildings. Those machines all use fossil fuels and release a lot of CO_2 into the air. And the way people get around can have a similar environmental impact. If cities are designed without allowing for public transportation (such as buses and subways), it means there will be more private cars on the road. And that means even more CO_2 in the atmosphere.

Cities can also create something called the urban heat island effect. The dark surfaces of roads, parking lots, and other paved areas absorb and then give off the Sun's heat. Ongoing construction and streets full of cars also produce heat. The problem is made even worse when natural areas are built over, and we lose the trees and plants that would have provided shade and cooler air. All this extra heat rises up to turn cities into hot "islands," which makes them uncomfortable to live in and adds to the warming of the entire planet.

The destruction of forests, meadows, creeks, and other ecosystems to make way for cities has also led to a loss of biodiversity. When they are deprived of their unique mix of native plants, animals, and insects, these natural areas become weakened and less able to survive a changing climate. For example, during the hottest months, an urban meadowland park wouldn't need to be watered as much as a mown field would, which saves a city's water supply.

Being part of a healthy ecosystem is also important for humans. For instance, like all animals, we rely on the oxygen that trees and other plants create to survive. As well, urban birds and animals become stressed and sick when they lose the natural areas that had given them shelter, paths for safe travel, places to hibernate, or been a source of the food they eat. There is a chance people will also get sick by coming into contact with these unwell animals.

The loss of biodiversity also affects our food security, which is our ability to access enough healthy food. If we can grow fruits and vegetables right in our cities (called urban agriculture), they will be fresher and less expensive. We'll also reduce the greenhouse gases that are produced when food is transported long distances. And when pollinator species, such as native bees, lose their habitat, the plants they pollinate will produce less food.

Another environmental concern is urban water, meaning *all* the water that falls (as rain

BIODIVERSITY describes the many different living things in a particular area, including even the smallest microscopic organisms that live in soil, in water, and on plants. An **ECOSYSTEM** is a community of living things, such as plants and animals, that interact with each other and with non-living things, such as water and soil, within a certain area. **POLLINATORS** are the insects and other animals that help plants reproduce by spreading pollen. They play a critical role in keeping an ecosystem thriving.

and snow, for example) and flows (through rivers and creeks) in a city, as well as the water that runs underground. This water is at risk of being polluted because cities around the world are experiencing intense and more frequent rainfall as a result of climate change.

Most cities have been designed with gray infrastructure that allows water from rain and snow to drain into pipes below the ground. Water is also absorbed naturally by green areas like meadows and forests. But what happens when these areas have been replaced by hard surfaces, such as paved roads and parking lots? The excess water from heavy or more frequent rain or snow has nowhere to go. This can cause flooding and, when older underground water management systems are overwhelmed, send pollutants, such as sewage and road salt, into natural water bodies.

But there is good news when it comes to urban areas and the environment! By looking to nature and including a variety of green infrastructure technologies when planning and designing our cities, we are helping to deal with the impacts of extreme storm events, rising temperatures, biodiversity loss, and other issues related to climate change. In other words, cities are becoming part of the solution, not just part of the problem.

CHAPTER 2

Nature First: *Creating Greener Cities*

You can find examples of nature in any city, from plants growing up through cracks in sidewalks to sharp-eyed birds flying overhead looking for their next meal. In the past, a city's green spaces might have included parks with trimmed hedges and trees, closely cut grass lawns, and fancy gardens for people to stroll through, but this kind of design didn't give enough thought to the needs of all the plants and creatures living there. In other words, city planning didn't always take into consideration how nature works and how humans can live in harmony with it.

Today, cities around the world are choosing to embrace nature and go green. A "green city" is one that is designed with green infrastructure to be part of the solution to climate change, not the cause of it. Green cities are better at dealing with extreme weather events, and they are also healthier, more comfortable places for people to live, work, and play alongside other creatures that make their homes there.

Take, Paris, France, for example. It wants to be the greenest city in Europe and has been taking action to get there. Now Parisians can enjoy streets just for walking and biking that have newly planted trees, green roofs, and rain gardens, as well as areas for urban agriculture and other spaces that have been allowed to grow wild. These steps have cleaned the air and water and made the city a more beautiful place to live. And the changes also helped fight climate change by cooling the air to counteract the dangerous heat waves Paris has experienced in recent years.

In China, some cities are using green infrastructure as part of a countrywide "sponge city" project. But how is a city like a sponge? When it has been designed to soak up and hold rainwater. Sponge cities use technologies like permeable pavement (walkways and parking lots that let water flow through to and be absorbed by the ground below), green roofs and gardens, and newly planted wetlands to deal with both flooding and serious water shortages.

You might hear people use the term **SUSTAINABLE CITIES** when they talk about climate change and the environment. Sustainability means meeting the needs of all living things today in a way that allows the same benefits for future generations too.

Learning from Indigenous Knowledge

An important and valuable way to support a green approach to city building is to respect and learn from Indigenous Knowledge. That's because it teaches us to see the world through a lens in which we are understood to be part of and related to nature, rather than in control of it.

This understanding has been passed down through countless generations of Indigenous Peoples and is unique to the places where it originated and evolved over thousands of years. For example, on Turtle Island (the name commonly used for North America by First Peoples), the phrase "all my relatives" is often shared to remind us that humans are related to all of nature. Earth is appreciated as Mother Earth, who provides everything for us and is our home, a place where everything has a right to live and a purpose for being.

When you understand that you are connected to *all* of nature, you begin to see things differently. For instance, you can appreciate water as living and life-giving, not just something to bathe or swim in. Or instead of being annoyed as bees buzz around you, you can remember how hard they work to pollinate the plants that become the food you eat. Understanding our relationship to nature in this way makes it easier for us to appreciate

"'As people disappear from sight, the Land remains.' This Māori proverb stresses the importance of respecting and preserving the land for future generations."

—JOSEPHINE CLARKE,
Māori landscape architect

our responsibility to Earth and to other living things that also call our planet home—and this includes how we think about designing and building our cities.

How governments can include Indigenous voices in the planning of green infrastructure can be seen in Aotearoa (a name for New Zealand given by Māori, the island country's Indigenous people). When the country first began building its cities, many years ago, Māori were not asked to be involved. But due to an important agreement made between the British government and Māori in 1840, the New Zealand government has now begun to work with Māori to include their perspective and unique knowledge to create greener cities that honor their culture.

In one recent example, a government study about urban water concluded that significant changes must be made to how cities collect and treat water in order to reflect Māori knowledge that water gives us life and that people need to protect it. Māori appreciate that humans need to care for nature to benefit both present and future generations, an understanding that is linked to the *mauri*, or the life pulse of the environment. Māori and other Indigenous Peoples around the world have always understood that there are important interconnections between all living things.

MĀORI traditionally use storytelling to share information and teachings, including the scientific knowledge important in designing green infrastructure. To people who are not Indigenous, it may seem strange to use stories as part of formal designs, but it is important to hear and respect this form of sharing information. Government projects are now also using *Te Reo Māori me ōna tikanga* (Māori language) in city plans and projects.

The Building Blocks of Green Infrastructure

When we talk about a city's green infrastructure, we mean both nature itself and the various technologies available to harness nature's powers. These include nature-based solutions for preventing flooding, reducing temperatures, improving air quality, removing greenhouse gases, and restoring biodiversity.

It might not be easy to go green right away, but many cities are finding ways to make more use of green infrastructure and to replace or

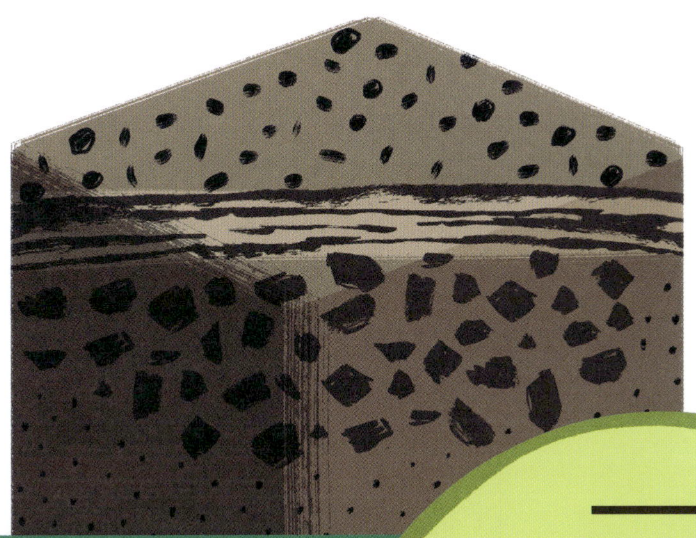

update gray infrastructure with green options. Some of these efforts might seem small on their own, but they have a big impact when they are made across a city and then a whole country!

To plan and build green cities, we must understand the characteristics and needs of green infrastructure's building blocks: water, soil, plants, and living creatures. Nature works as a collection of systems, with each part having special qualities that help them all work together.

"... the ancient wisdom of nature is ready to teach us that we are all connected in a web of life."

—DR. DIANA BERESFORD-KROEGER,
Botanist and medical biochemist

WATER

All creatures need water to live. And in cities, we also need to live *with* it. Understanding how water changes form (often throughout the seasons) and how it flows through urban spaces is an important part of green infrastructure.

The design of a city with green infrastructure takes into consideration the amazing way water takes three different forms as part of the natural water cycle: solid (snow and ice), liquid (rain and melted snow and ice), or gas (mist and fog). For example, a green-designed parking lot includes space for snow to collect, sloping surfaces for rain to drain off, and gardens with plants that absorb excess water up through their roots and release cooling evaporation into the air through the small holes in their leaves.

Managing the flow of liquid water and preventing it from being polluted is a particular concern for cities. A "watershed" is the area of land where water collects before eventually flowing to a larger body of water, such as a creek, river, or lake. The "stormwater" that flows into a watershed is rain or melted snow and ice that can't be absorbed into the ground.

A watershed also holds "groundwater" that flows deep between layers of rock under the Earth's surface. It's often used for the drinking water that fills wells or gets pumped up to large water tanks and eventually into peoples' homes. Groundwater needs to be protected from the pollutants that stormwater often picks up as it flows across city roads and other surfaces.

Traditional gray infrastructure, such as pipes and sewers, is built to catch and control the flow of water so that it will run off paved areas quickly. But green infrastructure is designed to also slow water's flow, absorb it, and filter pollutants out of it.

"We all need water. We wouldn't be able to live without water. Nothing would."

—AUTUMN PELTIER,
Ojibwe water advocate,
Wiikwemkoong Unceded Territory

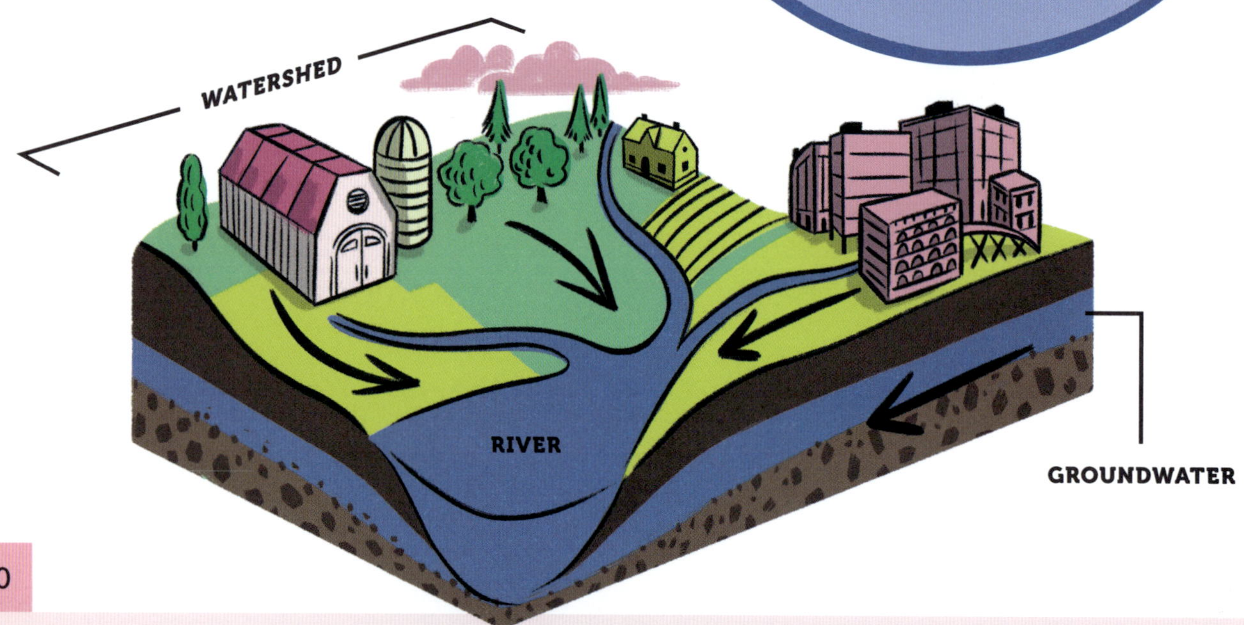

SOIL

When it comes to soil, there's much more than meets the eye. It's made mostly of tiny particles of broken rocks and minerals, combined with some organic matter from decaying plants, animals, and even poop. In fact, one teaspoonful of healthy soil contains up to a billion living microbes!

A soil's health depends on the mix of the particle sizes (this determines how well water is absorbed) and how much organic matter it contains (this adds needed nutrients for growing plants). How well the soil has been treated is also a factor. For example, if an area of land is constantly driven over by heavy vehicles, the soil will get packed down, making it harder for water, air, and even plant roots to move through it.

There are a number of reasons why soil matters to a city's green infrastructure. Trees and other plants need healthy soil to thrive. Soil also helps prevent urban flooding by acting like a sponge: the healthier it is, the better it can absorb and hold on to rainwater and stormwater, even under pavement! Soil also cleans stormwater by filtering out pollutants as the water runs through it. And it stores carbon—in the roots of plants, for example, and in the decaying bodies of dead animals. By holding on to carbon, soil helps reduce greenhouse gas emissions and address climate change.

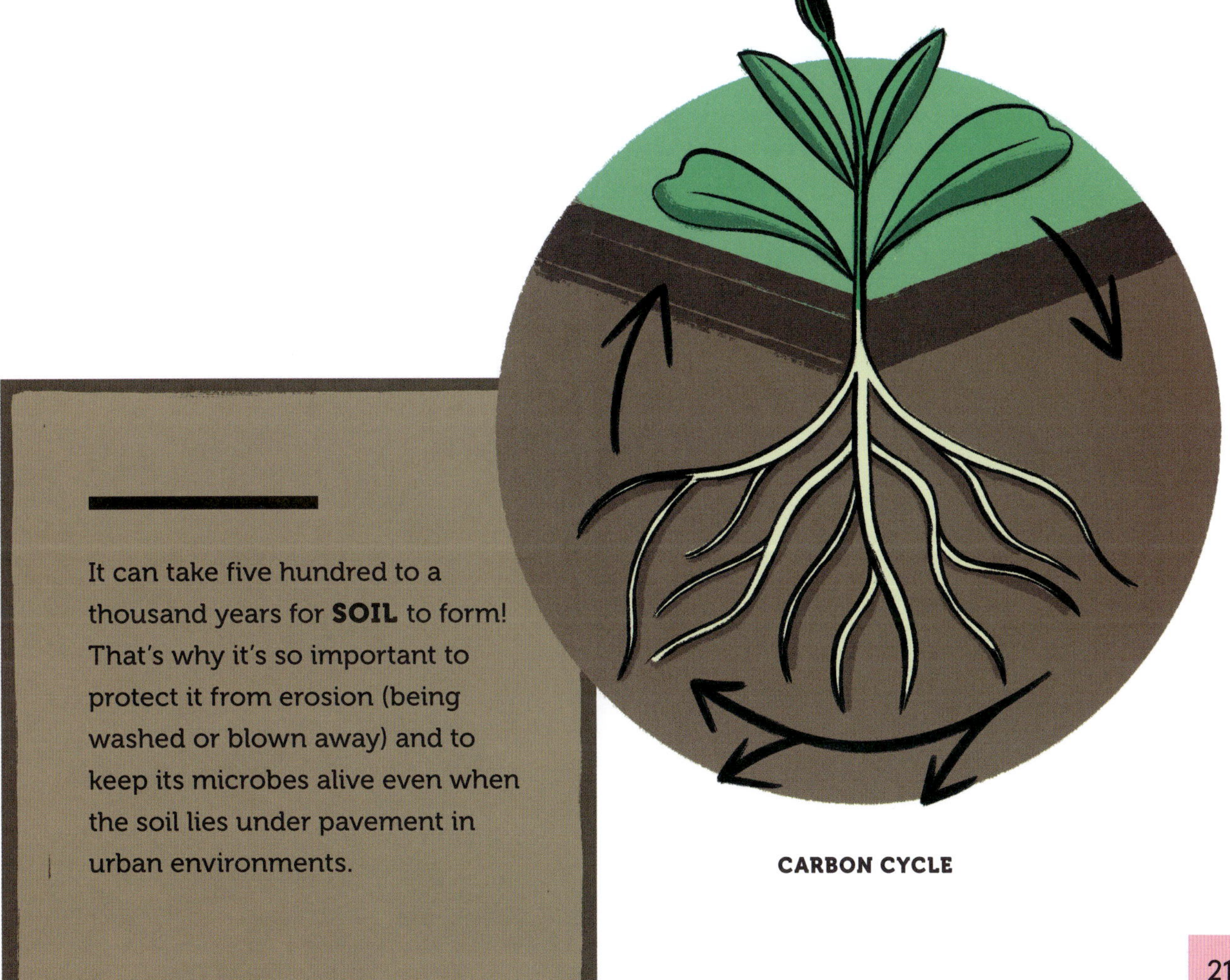

It can take five hundred to a thousand years for **SOIL** to form! That's why it's so important to protect it from erosion (being washed or blown away) and to keep its microbes alive even when the soil lies under pavement in urban environments.

CARBON CYCLE

PLANTS

Plants have been growing on Earth for about five hundred million years, and they are essential to our survival.

Through a process called photosynthesis, plants take carbon dioxide out of the air and release the oxygen that we and most other creatures need to breathe. They also provide habitats for many animals and can be used to make houses and other structures. Plants are sources of food and medicine too. In fact, Indigenous Peoples around the world know how to use local plants for medicine, and they respect plants as a critical part of the natural world to which we all belong.

Urban plants play a number of important roles in green infrastructure. In addition to removing CO_2 and other greenhouse gases from the atmosphere, trees and plants lessen the heat island effect by providing shade and putting moisture into the air. They also clean the air by trapping dust and other pollutants with their leaves. And they help manage stormwater because their leaves catch rain and their roots absorb water that has been captured by the soil.

When designing green infrastructure, it is important to include native plants. These are plants that naturally grow in a given area and have evolved to be ideally suited to grow there. Planting native species also adds biodiversity. Let's say, for instance, that a creature such as a wild bee eats the pollen of one particular kind of plant, and it also acts as a pollinator by moving from plant to plant as it eats. The native plant and the wild bee rely on each other to survive. If one species ceases to exist, the other probably will as well.

All the trees in a city make up what we call an **URBAN FOREST**. Even trees growing in the yards where people live belong to the urban forest. Together, city trees are an essential part of an urban ecosystem—they are often called the "lungs of cities" because of all the oxygen and clean air they provide.

CREATURES

Although we often think of wildlife as something that lives outside of a city, urban environments are home to countless creatures. Some animals have adapted to areas built on or near their natural habitats. Others have migrated or been transported to cities and have adapted to survive. In North America, most birds and squirrels have learned to share our urban spaces with us in broad daylight, but some urban animals, such as rats and raccoons, come out mainly at night. And city owls still fly at night looking for prey like mice, just as they do in a forest!

When an ecosystem has more creatures, it is more biodiverse, healthier, and better able to survive extreme weather events and diseases. A mown field of grass can be a habitat for certain kinds of insects, but a biodiverse garden that acts like a natural meadow supports a wide variety of pollinating bees and butterflies, birds, and small mammals.

Insects play a critical role in helping green infrastructure work. Along with birds and bats, they help plants reproduce by acting as pollinators. And when they poop or die, they add organic material and nutrients to the soil, making it a healthier place for plants to grow.

Larger animals, such as foxes, coyotes, and deer, need urban landscapes that are connected so they can move between natural spaces without having to cross dangerous roads and railway lines. Small mammals also need to be able to move freely across the land to find food and places to live. Cities can help by creating green infrastructure that protects and connects natural spaces. People can also be taught about the importance of biodiversity within urban spaces so we learn to work together to protect it.

Green infrastructure includes **WILDLIFE CROSSINGS**, such as bridges meant for animals (not vehicles) that are planted with trees and other plants. In the Netherlands, wildlife crossings are often found along canals.

CHAPTER 3

Going Green: *Green Infrastructure in Action*

It's clear why cities around the world are turning to green infrastructure: it's a way to address climate change; it makes cities stronger when dealing with the effects of climate change; and it makes cities healthier, more comfortable, and more enjoyable places to live.

But you're probably wondering what green infrastructure technologies look like and how they work. Here are some examples of the kinds of green infrastructure you might see around a city.

STREET TREES

Street trees are often planted in grassy areas between roads and sidewalks. Often they are surrounded by pavement, and sometimes they are planted in underground soil cells. These cells are made of recycled plastic and filled with healthy soil that helps tree roots grow. And when stormwater is directed into this soil, it is filtered and absorbed while it waters the trees!

URBAN FORESTS

Trees play a major role in keeping cities livable—from producing oxygen and cooling the air to protecting the soil. Street trees are also considered part of the urban forest. And to introduce even more trees into densely packed urban neighborhoods, a Japanese botanist named Akira Miyawaki came up with the idea of planting little forests, sometimes called Miyawaki forests. The trees are planted in areas that can be as small as a parking spot, so long as they have full sunlight for at least eight hours a day. Because of the tight space, the trees grow much closer together than they would in a natural forest. This helps to crowd out weeds, keep soil moist, and protect younger trees from high winds. Little forests are now being planted in cities across the world, often by people in the surrounding community.

RAIN GARDENS AND BIOSWALES

Rain gardens and bioswales catch and treat stormwater. A rain garden is a garden specifically designed to capture rainwater. The word "bioswale" comes from the Greek *bios* (meaning "life" or "living") and "swale," which is a long, narrow channel or indentation. Both of these landscape features are placed downhill from hard surfaces such as roofs, roads, and sidewalks so that water flows into them. And they both contain hardy native and urban-tolerant plants that can survive really dry and really wet weather.

What makes rain gardens and bioswales special is what you don't see! Imagine a garden that is layered, kind of like a cake. First there is the layer we see, which is made up of plants and rocks. Under that is a deep layer of soil mixed with sand to encourage drainage. This soil sits on top of a thin layer of small washed stones. Finally, there's a layer of large washed stones that the water can drain through and be stored below. This entire system can be very deep—the height of an average adult!

GREEN ROOFS

A biodiverse green roof filled with an assortment of native plants improves the local ecosystem by attracting a variety of birds and insects. It also helps lower urban heat, and soaks up stormwater, easing the pressure on the city's gray infrastructure. A green roof is a system of layers that support healthy plant growth. It's different from a rooftop garden, which is made up of plant pots and planters. There are also blue-green roofs. They are "blue" because rainwater temporarily stored below the soil layer is used to water the plants.

GREEN WALLS

Making a wall into a garden adds nature back into even the smallest of spaces inside or outside a building. The more plants, the cleaner and cooler the air. Green walls on the outside of a building can provide a home for urban wildlife, including birds and insects. Some cities have even planted green walls under busy roadways, where otherwise there would be nothing but concrete and cars.

STORMWATER PONDS

These urban ponds help to clean stormwater by giving it a place to sit for long enough that the heavier dirt and pollutants can settle to the bottom. Many years later, workers remove the polluted soil to keep it from reentering the urban water system. When stormwater ponds are also designed to be similar to natural wetlands, with shallow slopes and biodiverse plants, they also enhance biodiversity and become a source of drinking water and a habitat for wildlife.

PERMEABLE PAVEMENT

Urban areas with a lot of foot and car traffic need sidewalks and roads. That's where permeable pavement comes in. It's a surface that is hard enough to walk on but also "permeable" because water can flow through it. This can mean paved tiles separated by stone- or grass-filled gaps for stormwater to flow through, or porous concrete, asphalt, or even stone paving surfaces that are specially made with very tiny holes for stormwater to seep through. This sponge-like infrastructure can help cities avoid flooding after a heavy rainfall by letting water run into storage areas below.

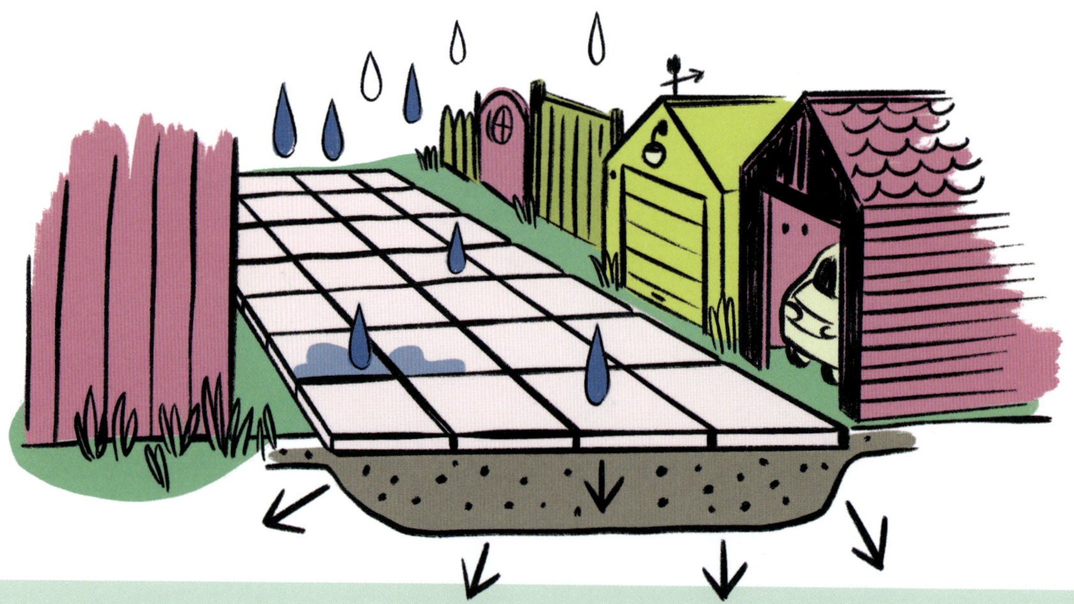

URBAN AGRICULTURE

Rooftop farms, community gardens, and food forests of fruit and nut trees that anyone can pick are all examples of urban agriculture. This is one way to improve food security in cities, especially in neighborhoods without grocery stores (also called food deserts). Urban agriculture also adds to a city's biodiversity and provides space for pollinating species to thrive. And communities prosper when their residents can buy local food directly from the people who grow it.

Imagine if a roof... became a farm!

BROOKLYN GRANGE, NEW YORK CITY, NEW YORK, UNITED STATES

When you walk through the busy concrete jungle of New York, you probably wouldn't expect to find a farmer's field. But look up and you might see one! Brooklyn Grange is a group of three rooftop farms that grow more than 100,000 lbs. (45,400 kg) of organic vegetables each year. Together, the farms cover an area about the size of three soccer fields!

A roof farm requires lots of rich soil that is deep enough to grow vegetables. And since roofs are often hot, dry, and windy, it also needs an irrigation system that collects rainwater and directs it to the plants through a series of small pipes.

Roof farms cover large areas. This means they are better at cooling the air and

absorbing carbon and rainwater than smaller green roofs. Their size also means more can be grown. Most food grown by the Brooklyn Grange is sold at farmers' markets in the community. Keeping it local means there's less need to transport fruits and vegetables long distances in trucks that emit harmful CO_2. The farms also give 60 percent of their harvest to organizations that help people who can't always afford fresh food, which is often more expensive than frozen or prepared food. And Brooklyn Grange has programs that teach people of all ages about urban agriculture, local ecology, and environmentally friendly initiatives for cities.

At one point, these were bare roofs serving only one purpose—to protect the building and spaces inside. As an urban farm, they are doing so much more!

Imagine if a hydro corridor . . . became a meadow trail!

THE MEADOWAY, TORONTO, ONTARIO, CANADA

A long path of mowed grass that runs under a corridor of hydro towers through a major city in Canada is being transformed. When it's finished, The Meadoway will be a 10 mi. (16 km) park made up of connected trails and rest areas. Not only that, but it will be home to over a thousand species of plants and creatures!

As often happens when cities are built and expanded, many of Toronto's natural habitats have been destroyed, including meadows that were once home to a variety of pollinators, such as bees, butterflies, birds, and small mammals. By bringing nature back

into otherwise unused land, The Meadoway will significantly add to the city's biodiversity, which is one of our best defenses against climate change.

Another benefit of having a naturally growing meadow filled with native plants is that it will no longer have grass that needs to be regularly mowed with large machines, and that means a decrease in the greenhouse gas emissions being produced by the city.

Long, narrow parks like The Meadoway are also called wildlife corridors. They give wild animals paths to travel safely throughout Toronto, away from neighborhoods and the danger of busy traffic. And one final benefit is that the people who live and work in the city have a beautiful biodiverse park filled with life that is easy to visit.

Imagine if a building ... became a vertical forest!

BOSCO VERTICALE, MILAN, ITALY

In central Milan, two high-rises are literally green buildings! The Bosco Verticale ("vertical forest" in Italian) is a complex that's home to humans, trees, plants, birds, and other living creatures.

Built in 2014, the two towers have become symbols of Milan and its efforts to be a greener city. The buildings were designed to add trees back into the city to fight the deforestation caused by Milan's growth and expansion. Also, by building up instead of out—in other words, constructing tall towers where many people can live rather than taking up much more land to build enough houses for the same number of people—the city ensured fewer natural areas were lost.

The buildings have larger and stronger balconies that can support all the soil and water needed to grow plants, as well as the weight of the plants themselves!

The vegetation in the two towers—which includes roughly eight hundred trees, five thousand shrubs, and fifteen thousand other plants—is equivalent to a forest about the size of seven American football fields. The plants thrive with the help of a central watering system that pumps groundwater from below the buildings using solar energy. And in only a few years, the buildings have increased the city's biodiversity by becoming home to about sixteen hundred birds and butterflies!

The leaves from the trees and plants create shade to make the living spaces inside the buildings more comfortable on hot sunny days. And the water that evaporates from the leaves helps cool the surrounding environment. The leaves also improve air quality by trapping pollutants and decrease the noise pollution that's part of life in a busy city.

But even sky forests need a little help. Once a year, a team of specially trained flying gardeners use mountain-climbing gear to scale the buildings to prune and check the health of the trees and shrubs.

Imagine if a schoolyard ... became a wetland!

PYMMES BROOK, LONDON, ENGLAND

A group of residents in north London were worried about the health of Pymmes Brook, a stream that runs through the area. Heavier rainfall due to climate change and an increase in paved surfaces thanks to urbanization meant the brook kept flooding. The solution? To "rewild" it back to its natural wetland state.

As part of the plan, computer modeling was used to show how wetlands could trap and filter out pollution from stormwater that was flowing into the brook. That's how schoolyards became part of the picture. A national conservation charity worked with students from ten local schools to design ways to transform areas in their schoolyards into wetlands. Teachers made this information part

What exactly is a **WETLAND**? Its name kind of says it all—it is an area of land that's covered by water at least part, if not all, of the year. Marshes and swamps are examples of these special ecosystems. They are home to both land and water plants and animals.

of the students' studies, and everyone was involved in the planting.

Like naturally occurring wetlands, these human-made wetlands are beneficial to the surrounding area and the people who live there. They have become home to a variety of urban wildlife, such as frogs, butterflies, dragonflies, and birds. Wetlands also help to cool the air by providing shade from the trees and additional moisture from the plants. And like any plant-filled environment, they store carbon in the rich earth they are made of.

And best of all, these wetland schoolyards are living laboratories for kids to connect with wildlife and learn about nature's systems.

Imagine if an old highway... became a public park!

SEOULLO 7017 SKYGARDEN, SEOUL, SOUTH KOREA

What does a city do with a highway that is no longer needed for vehicles? If that city is Seoul, the answer is to transform it into a public park filled with native plant species.

The soaring Seoullo 7017 Skygarden is an arboretum (a garden designed for educational purposes) floating high over the city. It has 645 tree pots that contain over 24,000 trees, shrubs, and other plants—all of which are organized in alphabetical order. The Skygarden is a kind of plant library, and each tree or shrub has a sign with information on it to help people learn more about the species. Some of the trees and shrubs grow edible

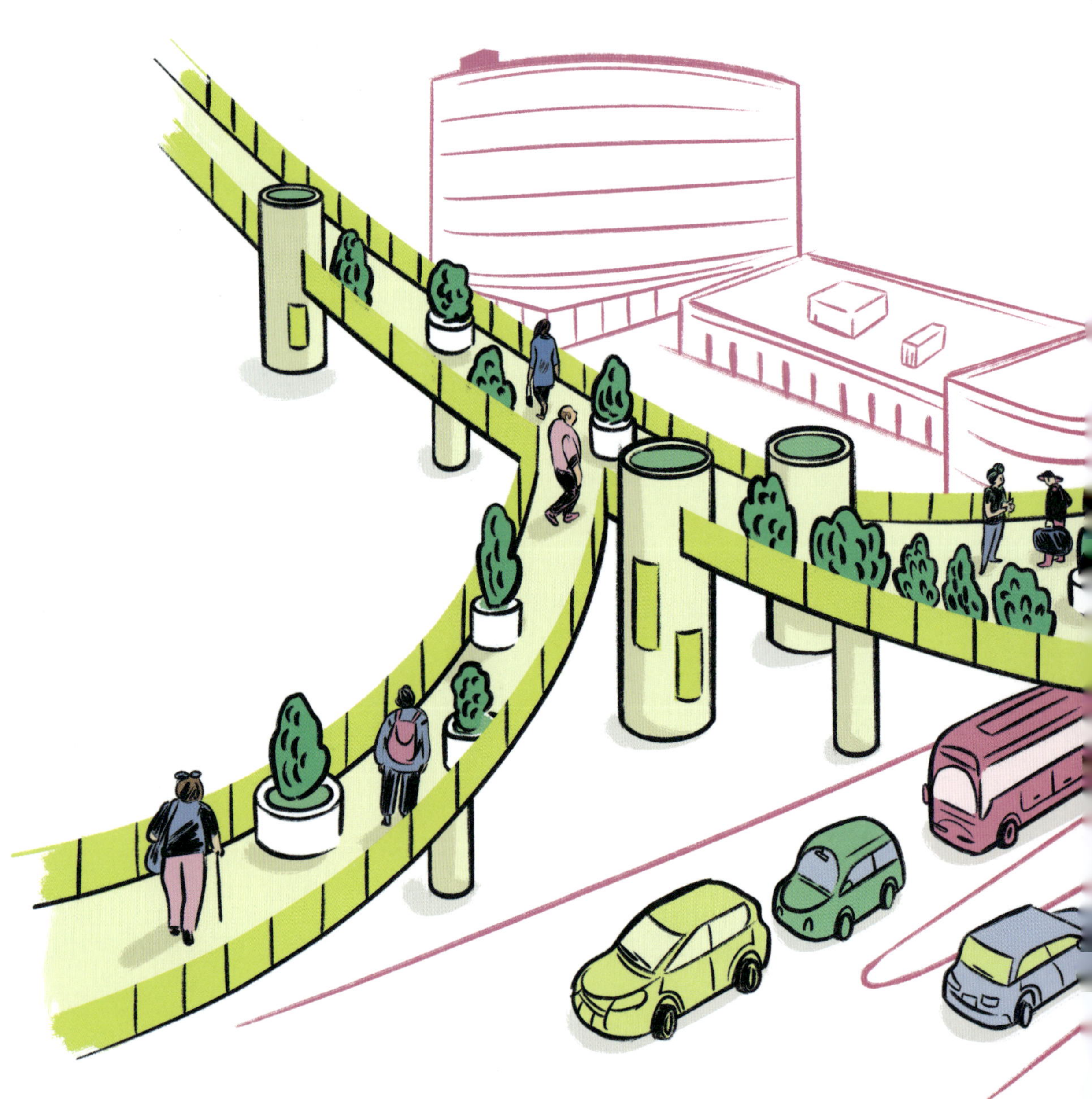

fruit. There's also a pond with floating water lilies, a large public square with fragrant rose gardens, another square with magnolia trees, a stage, and an outdoor café. The Skygarden is reachable by stairs, bridges, escalators, and motorized lifts so that everyone is able to enjoy the experience.

This project has been so successful that it has inspired more green infrastructure—like small gardens, green roofs, and even green streets—to make the surrounding area more eco- and pedestrian-friendly. Also, it tries to inspire people from across the city to learn about native plants and create new gardens of their own to make Seoul a greener place to live and work.

Imagine if a shipyard . . . became a rewilded neighborhood!

Bo01, MALMÖ, SWEDEN

What was once an old abandoned shipyard covered with contaminated soil is now a nature-filled neighborhood in one of Sweden's biggest cities. Bo01 was designed to improve access to nature for all—humans and nonhumans alike—by creating small, connected, and biodiverse green spaces within a heavily urban area. The word *bo* means "to dwell" (live) in Swedish, and 01 is short for 2001, the year the project was created.

Bo01 is Sweden's first carbon-neutral neighborhood, meaning its buildings add little to no carbon to the atmosphere. How? The houses use clean energy that is generated by windmills and are warmed by geothermal pumps that carry heat up from deep underground.

If you were to walk or bike around Bo01 (many of the roads are closed to cars), you

would see colorful gardens and small parks filled with native plants, as well as apartment buildings with green roofs. Throughout the neighborhood, there are spaces specially made to catch and direct stormwater, such as stone and grass channels and long gardens.

There are also areas designed to encourage more biodiversity, like human-made wetlands and planted native trees. Apartment building courtyards are alive with salamanders, frogs, and several species of bats. A saltwater canal is also a special habitat for fish, shellfish, and other aquatic life. Birdhouses support biodiversity and habitat as well, and now a number of seabird species have moved into the area and are raising their young there.

Imagine if an urban forest ... became a nature reserve!

KARURA FOREST RESERVE, NAIROBI, KENYA

In the northern part of Nairobi, Kenya's capital city, there is an actual forest. The Karura Forest covers a very large area: 2,500 acres (1,012 hectares) of land. Within the forest, there are rivers, a waterfall, and many historic caves.

As the city grew up around the Karura Forest, the government made it a protected area in 1932. Still, land developers wanting to illegally build housing tried to take over parts of the forest in the 1990s. But the forest thrives today thanks to the community activists who protected it. The late Dr. Wangari Maathai received a Nobel Peace Prize in 2004 for leading many of these efforts, and she is now credited with founding the Green Belt Movement. As part of this movement, women work with their communities to plant trees, protect the environment, and improve the lives of all people.

Many efforts continue to keep the Karura Forest a healthy ecosystem. For instance, the many non-native plants (likely brought in by humans) have been replaced so that almost three-quarters of the area is now covered with native species.

The Karura Forest plays an important role as green infrastructure for the city. Natural areas provide important environmental benefits to urban areas, including by acting as the "lungs" of a city by absorbing CO_2 and providing clean oxygen. And the forest is a popular spot, with about sixteen thousand visitors a month learning how nature supports a large city. A group of volunteers called the Friends of Karura Forest lead tours that teach people about ecological systems, birdwatching and animal tracking, the history and culture of the area, and the management and care of the forest.

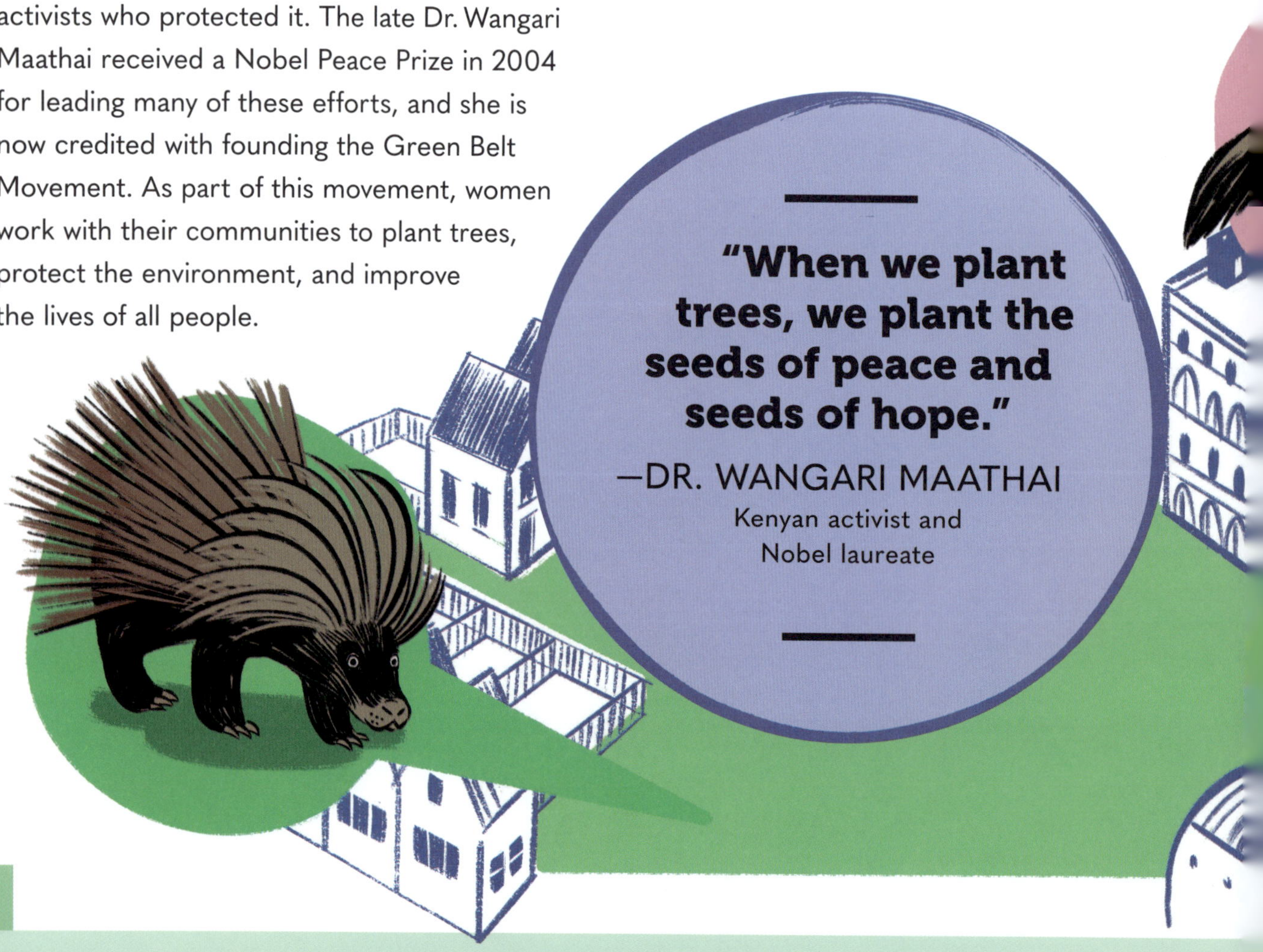

"When we plant trees, we plant the seeds of peace and seeds of hope."

—DR. WANGARI MAATHAI

Kenyan activist and Nobel laureate

Imagine if a desert city . . . became filled with mini-forests!

AMMAN MINI-FOREST, AMMAN, JORDAN

An industrial neighborhood in Amman, Jordan's capital city, might not be the first place you think of when you imagine a forest. But that is exactly where you will find a thriving mini-forest! And it's actually just one of a number of mini-forests that have been planted around the city.

Inspired by Akira Miyawaki and his tiny forests, the designers of this project have turned unused spaces across Amman, including one location that used to be a garbage dump, into tiny shade-producing forests. Part of their goal is to bring back the native trees that grew in these areas before the land was urbanized. These heat-resistant trees can survive in Jordan's dry landscape.

Although the mini-forests are each only about the size of a tennis court, they help lower the intense heat of the city, making life there more comfortable for humans and other creatures. Because of climate change, temperatures in the Middle East are rising almost twice as quickly as they are in other places around the world. But under the canopy of a mini-forest, the temperature can be over 22°F (12°C) cooler than in the sun!

These mini-forests are also making a big difference to the environmental health of the neighborhoods they are planted in, and they have created habitats for the local wildlife, such as butterflies, birds, and even foxes. And the closely planted trees—an important part of the Miyawaki approach—also help block the harsh desert winds and are more resistant to forest fires, which is a big concern in hot climates.

Imagine if a deforested country . . . became reforested!

REFORESTING INDIA, INDIA

With a population of over 1.4 billion people, India has lost many of its natural forests to the demand for firewood, pastureland, and urban space. Recently, though, the country's government has promised to plant enough trees to cover at least one-third of the country!

By growing millions of native species, including in its many cities, India can reduce its climate change contribution in important ways: by removing CO_2 and pollutants from the air, adding biodiversity, improving water quality, reducing flooding, and decreasing urban heat. In fact, the densely populated city of Mumbai has been recognized globally for its efforts to plant and care for urban trees.

Here's the plan that Mumbai followed: Over eighty different species of small trees were given to government workers, citizens, schools, and businesses to be planted as urban forests, as well as alongside roads and railway lines. Schoolchildren were also asked to create artwork to explain the importance of the tree-planting program.

In the northern state of Uttar Pradesh, 220 million trees have been planted—one for each person who lives there. In one twenty-four-hour period, more than 50 million trees were planted, breaking a world record! Elsewhere around the country, villages have made their tree-planting events symbols of cultural importance. For instance, in Piplantri, Rajasthan, 111 trees are planted for every baby girl born, to remind people of the importance of women to society.

Since the trees need to thrive after they've been planted, scientists use technology to keep track of each one. The holes where the trees are planted are geotagged, and the saplings are given QR codes. The trees are also monitored using aerial photography, which can show if they are healthy or need extra care. The Forest Survey of India found that forest cover has now reached a quarter of the country—over 870 sq. mi. (2,260 sq km)!

A well-known **INDIAN PROVERB** says, "Blessed is he who plants trees under whose shade he will never sit." This means that it's important to thank people who plant the trees that will benefit future generations.

Making Our Future Even Greener

—THE GREEN TEAM—

It takes a large team of specially trained people working together to plan, build, and care for a green city. Below are some of the key professions involved in creating green infrastructure. Maybe you can imagine yourself doing one of these jobs someday.

LANDSCAPE ARCHITECTS design outdoor environments for cities and other spaces that take into account how humans use spaces and what nature needs to thrive. They design outdoor areas on and around buildings, including rooftop terraces and green roofs. They also design systems to contain soil and manage stormwater so it flows into specially created landscaped areas.

ENGINEERS design infrastructure, such as roads, bridges, and sewer systems. Some engineers are responsible for the structural aspects, such as the road systems, and others for the mechanical systems, such as drains on roofs, helping with green infrastructure designs. There are also engineers that specialize in electrical projects, such as lighting in parks and on streets.

ARBORISTS help trees grow and thrive in harsh urban environments. They monitor the health of trees, advise ways to keep them healthy, and sometimes cut branches that are dying or at risk of falling off.

ARCHITECTS design buildings, taking into consideration how they will be used, what they will look like, and what materials they will be made of. They work with civil engineers to ensure that their designs are buildable and safe. They also work closely with landscape architects.

CITY PLANNERS (also known as urban planners) design communities that are safe and comfortable to live in. When creating their plans, they work with citizens to understand their needs, and they consider things like how land will be used, how built-up the area will be, how many people it will need to support, and what infrastructure is required. They make sure that all plans follow each individual city's regulations, and they design and advocate for green infrastructure.

URBAN ECOLOGISTS are scientists who study city ecosystems and the relationship between humans and other species living there. They look for ways humans can live in harmony with nature, and they offer ideas to make cities greener.

URBAN FORESTERS focus on how to plan, protect, and care for all the trees in a city. They also work closely with city planners and arborists to make sure that the health of urban trees is monitored, and they advise on ways to improve conditions for city forests.

How Can You Help Now?

Building green cities takes a lot of work on the part of *many* people of all ages. And that means you too! While you might not be the one making the decision to put a green roof on the apartment building where you live or transform a hydro corridor into a meadow park, you can play a role in making sure green initiatives around your city are successful.

Here are some ways that you and your friends can get involved:

- Join or start an **ECOTEAM** that finds ways to help nature thrive around your school and in your neighborhood. One way to do this is to create maps that show where the big trees and green spaces are in your community and include ideas for adding in new green infrastructure, such as planting native trees in your schoolyard or creating a rain garden where rainwater is already flowing (for example, from the downspouts off a roof). Then use these maps when you talk to your parents or teachers about making these actions a reality.
- Volunteer at **COMMUNITY PLANTING** events that restore local ecosystems, and talk to people about how green infrastructure can support these spaces.
- Help out at an **URBAN FARM**. You can do things like move soil and compost, plant, weed, mulch, and harvest. Yum!
- Stories help cities too, so learn about yours! Since 1995, the Toronto Green Community has been taking people on **STORYTELLING TOURS** of the city's buried creeks. These "Lost Rivers" talks encourage people to think about their personal role in protecting and improving urban water systems.
- Look for examples of **GREEN INFRASTRUCTURE** in your neighborhood and keep an eye on how they are doing. Write down what you see and draw pictures as well. For example, if your city has planted a bioswale or rain garden but the plants are looking unhealthy or water is pooling, ask an adult to report it to the city so the problem can be fixed.
- Become a **CITIZEN SCIENTIST** by signing up for environmental programs that teach you how to study and document your local urban ecosystem. You can "adopt" nearby green infrastructure to study. The information you record can help urban ecologists understand if an area is diverse enough, if water is draining properly, and if there are changes in the plant and animal species living and growing there.

THE WORLD WILDLIFE FUND (WWF) AND THE GLOBAL YOUTH BIODIVERSITY NETWORK are two of many international environmental organizations helping young people get involved in conservation and enhancing biodiversity that also supports green infrastructure.

For example, the WWF's Green Generation Club is aimed at eight- to fourteen-year-olds living in ten villages in the Tanintharyi Region of Myanmar, a country that is extremely vulnerable to natural disasters caused by climate change. Twenty trained educators from the community lead projects focused on the preservation of forests, rivers, and wildlife, as well as water conservation and waste reduction.

And in Canada, the WWF runs a Bioblitz program that brings together people of all ages to search for and document how species live in a certain area at the same time each year. The information is analyzed and made available to everyone, and it's especially helpful in planning and caring for ecosystems that are at risk because of urbanization.

GREEN INFRASTRUCTURE creates cities with landscapes that help slow the effects of climate change, as well as cities that are healthier and more comfortable places to live. It means people breathe fresher air, stormwater runs cleaner, and urban insects, birds, and animals live better lives too.

Urban environments are always being built and rebuilt, so planning for green infrastructure means we can change the rules of the game and design cities that are more resilient and biodiverse. From vertical forests to rewilded schoolyards, there's a lot happening around the world that proves there are better, greener ways to build cities. And as the Miyawaki mini-forests show us, even small changes can make a difference when they are repeated and scaled up! By sharing your understanding of what green infrastructure is and how it works, you can play a part in the green cities of the future.

Of course, if we want our cities to be greener, we'll have to make some difficult choices and have some tough conversations. For example, we need to question our ideas of a beautiful landscape. Is it a mowed grass lawn and weedless garden, or the "messy" look of a biodiverse meadow filled with native plants and pollinating insects? In some parts of our cities, we have changed the land so much that native

plants can't survive there anymore. Some urban ecologists feel that some non-native plants can be planted in these areas because they can provide environmental benefits such as cooling the air and absorbing stormwater. But others feel strongly that to better support biodiversity, we should only grow native plants, no matter what.

Cities that include green infrastructure bring humans into closer contact with plants, soil, waterways, and creatures. Having a relationship with nature is now widely appreciated for having many healing benefits. There are even horticultural therapists who design gardens meant to help improve mental health, or help ill people feel better by connecting with plants and soil. Healing gardens are designed for people to explore, rest in, walk through, meditate in, and also to gather and spend time with others.

Around the world, people (like you!) are learning about green infrastructure. By coming together and applying this knowledge, we are creating beautiful places that say—to all of nature—"we want and need you here too."

GLOSSARY

BIODIVERSITY: The many different living things in a particular area, including even the smallest microscopic organisms that live in soil, in water, and on plants.

CITY: A large built-up area where many people live close together. Also called urban centers.

CITY PLANNING: The process of creating a long-term overall design for a city, including its infrastructure.

CLIMATE CHANGE: The collective long-term shifts in the average temperatures and weather patterns of a region due to increased global heat.

ECOSYSTEM: A community of living things, such as plants and animals, that interact with each other and with non-living things, such as water and soil, within a certain area.

GRAY INFRASTRUCTURE: An approach to city building that relies on technologies, such as bridges and pipes, typically made out of human-made materials, such as concrete, metal, or plastic.

GREEN INFRASTRUCTURE: A nature-based approach to city building that works with natural systems and processes to prevent and lessen the effects of climate change while also supporting biodiversity.

HEAT ISLAND EFFECT: An effect that happens when the buildings and paved surfaces in cities absorb and retain heat (from the Sun or vehicle motors, for example), which is trapped and causes increased overall temperatures.

INFRASTRUCTURE: The systems and facilities that ensure a city functions well.

NATIVE SPECIES: A plant or animal species that originated and developed in its surrounding habitat and is uniquely adapted to living in that particular environment.

PERMEABLE: A type of material that allows liquids or gases to pass through it.

POLLINATORS: The insects and other animals that help plants reproduce by spreading pollen and that play a critical role in keeping ecosystems healthy.

SUSTAINABLE: Meeting the needs of all living things today in a way that allows the same benefits for future generations.

URBANIZATION: The process by which large numbers of people move to and live in relatively small areas to form towns and cities.

WETLAND: A special ecosystem made up of an area of land that is covered by water at least part, if not all, of the year.

SELECTED SOURCES

Bell, Nicole, Kim Wheatley, and Bob Johnson. *The Ways of Knowing Guide: Earth's Teachings*. Toronto: Toronto Zoo with Turtle Island Conservation, 2012. Online.

Beresford-Kroeger, Diana. *The Global Forest: 40 Ways Trees Can Save Us*. Toronto: Penguin Books, 2010.

Biswas, Asit K., and Kris Hartley. "China's 'Sponge Cities' Aim to Re-use 70% of Rainwater: Here's How." *The Conversation*, September 5, 2017. Online

Canadian Wildlife Federation. "Why We Bioblitz!" Online.

CBC.ca. "I Am Indigenous: Autumn Peltier." YouTube.

Corbley, Andy. "India's Mass Tree-Planting Success: Forest Cover Grows by Half-Million Acres in Two Years." Good News Network, February 15, 2022. Online.

David Suzuki Foundation. "What Is Climate Change?" Online.

Goodall, Jane, with Phillip Berman. *Reason for Hope: A Spiritual Journey*. New York: Warner Books, 1999.

Kroze, Harvey. "Karura Forest: More Than Just a Pleasant Walk in the Woods." *Swara*, November 11, 2016. Online.

Let's Talk Science. "What Is Soil?" September 21, 2019. Online.

Robinson, Amanda. "Turtle Island." *The Canadian Encyclopedia*. Historica Canada. November 6, 2018. Online.

Tayseer, Mohammad, and Laura Millan. "Fast-Growing Mini Forests Help Cool Down a Desert City." Bloomberg, August 30, 2023. Online.

Te Tiriti o Waitangi Treaty of 1840, signed by Māori and the British government: www.waitangitribunal.govt.nz/en/about/the-treaty/about-the-treaty

Wagamese, Richard. *One Drum: Stories and Ceremonies for a Planet*. Madeira Park, BC: Douglas & McIntyre, 2019.

World Wildlife Fund. Green Generation Club Online.

INDEX